40424621R00061

Made in the USA
Lexington, KY
29 May 2019